OUT OF THE SHADOWS

A Story of Toni Wolff and Emma Jung

OUT OF THE SHADOWS

A Story of Toni Wolff and Emma Jung

by Elizabeth Clark-Stern

Genoa House

Published by
Genoa House
www.genoahouse.com
books@genoahouse.com
1-888-298-9717 Toll free Canada & the US
+1-831-298-5335 International

Out of the Shadows: A Story of Toni Wolff and Emma Jung
Copyright © 2010 Elizabeth Clark-Stern
ISBN 978-0-9813939-4-0
First Edition

Published simultaneously in Canada, the United Kingdom, and the United States of America. For information on obtaining permission for use of material from this work, please submit a written request to: books@genoahouse.com

Out of the Shadows is a work of creative imagination, based on real events. The playwright acknowledges research drawn from the works of C.G. Jung, Emma Jung, Toni Wolff, Marie-Louise von Franz, Barbara Hannah, Murray Stein, James Hillman, Jean Shinoda Bolen, Marion Woodman, and *Jung* by Dierdre Bair.

Distributed by
Fisher King Books
PO Box 222321
Carmel, CA 93922
+1-831-238-7799
1-800-228-9316 Toll Free Canada & USA

Acknowledgment to the Seattle Jung Society, the Northwest Alliance for Psychoanalytic Study, and the Mother House Fund for the devotion and sponsorship that made this work possible. And to my dear, ebullient therapist/artist colleagues, Catherine Sprietsma Adler, Robin McCoy Brooks, and the original cast and crew and consultants, for their creativity, collaboration and loving support.

ORIGINAL CAST:

EMMA JUNG. Rikki Ricard

TONI WOLFF. Elizabeth Clark-Stern

Directed by. Shierry Nicholsen

Project Sponsor/Artistic Consultant. Lee Roloff

Sound Operator. Donna Lee

Sound Recording. Brent Robinette

Photography, Media. John Stern

Consultants. Susan Scott, Janet Smith, Paul Collins

Music selected by the author from the works of Bach, Debussy, Finzi, Mozart, Ravel, Prokofiev, and Shostakovich

CHARACTERS:

EMMA JUNG (1882-) ages from 26 to 71 years

TONI WOLFF (1888-) ages from 22 to 65 years

SETTING:

The Jung family home, 228 Seestrasse Küsnacht, Switzerland:
Kitchen
Garden
Carl Jung's study
Emma Jung's study
Hotel Room, Ravenna, Italy
Outside the door of Jung's hospital room, Zürich
Gemeindestrasse, home of the C.G. Jung Institute

TIME: 1910-1953

ACT ONE: 1910-1918

ACT TWO: 16 years later 1934-1953

ACT ONE

MUSIC in the darkness.

LIGHTS UP on EMMA, looking out at the audience as she addresses her memory of Toni.

EMMA

How many times did I see you, Toni Wolff, whispering up the path, the pearl buttons of your lace blouse catching the morning sun? At first I saw a face, a voice, a turn of the chin, bemusement in those eyes. I remember the slenderness of your body, your hair sculpted in waves beneath a stylish French hat. Sometimes you wore it pulled into a tight knot like a coiled snake. You came laden with books, or your father's chess set, a flutter of sweat and cigarettes. I carried the roses. Remember? In the beginning, you looked up to me with the eyes of a child, that first morning in the moist summer of 1910.

MUSIC.

EMMA exits.

TONI enters The Garden.

EMMA *(off stage)*

Franzlie, please do not eat them all! I need one full pail for the raspberry pie

EMMA enters, flowers in her apron.

EMMA

Eck! You gave me such a fright.

TONI

Forgive me.

3

EMMA

> My husband's new analysand.

TONI

> Is that a term coined by Dr. Sigmund Freud?

EMMA

> No, but my husband is a close professional colleague of Dr. Freud's.
>
> *(extending her hand)*
>
> I am Emma Jung.

TONI *(shaking hands)*
Antonia Wolff.

EMMA

> A firm grip for one so young.

TONI

> I am twenty-two.

EMMA

> Are you married?

TONI

> "It is an honor that I dream not of."

EMMA

> Shakespeare! Be careful what you denounce. Juliet was soon "fast married."

TONI

> I longed to go to University. My father forbade it. I was sent to England to be "finished" in a school of manners for fine ladies. Now, he is dead and there is nothing left for me.

EMMA

> I grieved to hear of his passing. One of the finest families in Switzerland. You and your mother, your sisters, must be quite distraught.

TONI

> My sisters will marry. They know their course. I rage at my father. I alone was allowed into his study. He opened for me the world of the Greeks, Shakespeare. But I was born female. A son he would have sent to University. What am I to do now, Papa, with this mind you tended?

EMMA

> Did my husband agree to treat you?

TONI

> I have not seen him yet. This is my mother's idea.

EMMA

> Dr. Jung will not bite your head off.

TONI

> I was told he would—is that not the heart of analysis?

EMMA

> Perhaps, for Dr. Freud. My husband believes in sitting closer to his analysands, out from behind the couch, as it were.

TONI

> I will never see my father again, sit with him in the twilight, hear his voice reading Schiller, Strindberg. We took the part of each character in A DOLLS HOUSE. His mind, Ibsen's, and mine. There is nothing for me now but marriage to some dreary man I will despise

—as if I would ever give over the legal ownership of my fortune to such a husband. Wretched Swiss law.

EMMA

Come, my dear. Dr. Jung's study is straight up the path.

(offering a cutting from her apron)

Rosemary.

TONI

"For remembrance"?

EMMA

I predict no watery grave, for you, Ophelia.

TONI

Why not?

EMMA

The vigor of your handshake, my dear, your ruthless mind. You are too curious to commit suicide.

TONI

Pardon me, Frau Jung, but I believe you have not read sufficient Nietzsche. Have you a cigarette?

EMMA

With four children? I do not have sufficient time to smoke.

TONI

I will not endure this "talking cure"!

EMMA is silent.

I am leaving now.

EMMA waits.

TONI

> There is nothing before me but darkness—

EMMA holds her ground, waiting.

MUSIC.

EMMA exits.

TONI steps forward, facing the audience as she speaks to "Jung."

TONI

> With all due respect, Dr. Jung, Plato did not say that, it was Heraclitis. You certainly do care who said it. That is plainly evident by the riot of books surrounding you like a great tidal wave. Outstrips my father's library by a league. Heraclitis? I am proved correct. I must admit I am intrigued by your concept of the "psyche," Greek for soul. Your notion of the "Unconscious" as a vast undiscovered country within each of us. Seems quite fantastic, frankly, but you claim there is empirical evidence such a place exists? My father? What about him? My dreams? Of course I remember them! "And in dreaming, the clouds methought would open and show riches ready to drop upon me, that when I waked, I cried to dream again." My father read it to me. One of his favorite passages. He came to me last night in a dream so real I could feel the soft texture of his hospital gown. "Give me a cigarette," he said. I lighted it for him. He took the smoke deep into his lungs, whispering, "My Antonia, people when they live on this earth, they don't know what they have." What did he mean by that, Dr. Jung? You know the answer, but you believe I must discover it for myself. I have trespassed too long on your valuable time. Good day. What? For me?

A smooth stone from your Lake? How will this ease my mourning? That too I must discover for myself. You are not at all what I expected.

MUSIC.

TONI exits.

EMMA enters, sits at her table, holds up a letter, from which she reads aloud.

EMMA

Dear Professor Freud. Usually I am quite at one with my fate, and see very well how lucky I am. But from time to time I am tormented by the conflict of how I can hold my own against Carl. I find I have no friends. All the people who associate with us really only want to see Carl, except for a few quite uninteresting persons. I am instantly cordoned off as "the wife" and begin to doubt that I have any existence of my own, apart from the aura of Dr. Jung. I write to you because I know I have not come into my own. Carl has conducted an analysis of me, and trained me in his method, but I cannot begin my own practice with four children and a household to manage. I wonder if there is not something I can contribute to this burgeoning field that is my own.

(aside)

Eck, I am a whining haus frau—"Please great Dr. Freud, tell me I am important!"—Surely I ascribe too much greatness to this man, who towers like the Alps, so inflexible is his countenance. I see him with Carl, they are like a mountain and a river. Freud seemingly made of stone, yet one senses a hidden fluid nature underground. Carl is a rushing torrent that roars over hills and valleys, flowing beyond the solid rock of custom and country at his very core. And what am I? A pleasant meadow strewn with white daisies? Why is it not enough, to be Carl's wife, mother of his children, baker of his bread? I have a fine mind. Freud sees it. Why not my husband? Why can I not be Carl's Intellectual Muse?

MUSIC.

TONI enters, sits in The Garden. EMMA moves from her table to The Garden.

EMMA

Fraulein Wolff, you catch me in my fishing dress.

TONI

I dawdle. It is so lovely here.

EMMA

It is a wretched day. Haze covers the lake. The children wanted to catch a fish for lunch. We managed some fingerlings. You are waiting to see him?

TONI

No. I am collecting myself. We have been working all morning.

EMMA

All morning! You must be quite fatigued, my dear.

TONI

On the contrary. I feel fatigue when I am away from here.

EMMA

The feelings come rushing back, unbidden?

TONI

> The feelings roar on and off, like the weather, no matter. No. It is the exhaustion I feel when returning to ordinary life. I struggle to make a bridge from this sea journey of the mind, back to a world where I must preside at my mother's dinner table, order food for the cook, pretend to everyone that my existence is of only one dimension. I long to return to this place where he unravels meaning from my dreams like a cat pulling threads of yarn from a sweater—from that place, I see a new world. The substance of a "me" I have never known.

EMMA

> Such riches are being revealed to you.

TONI

> I dream nightly, images that come and go as if I am seeing them through fine English lace. I wake and think, was that the silhouette of a tree rising from a barren landscape—or the shadow of someone I once knew, reaching her arms out into the wilderness? Even in waking life I have the sensation of roiling forces, things shattering, cracking open—

EMMA

> What did my husband say of this?

TONI

> Come five times a week!

EMMA

> He is quite devoted to you.

TONI

> I do not trust it. The "doubting Thomas" in me thinks Dr. Jung is out to suck on my family fortune, but

everyone knows of your of your considerable wealth, so what would be his motive, but to help me?

EMMA

You comprehend a great deal for one so young, one who has not lived in the world outside her family home.

TONI

Your world is quite vast, Frau Jung. Hosting Albert Einstein for dinner - what it must have been like for you to swim in the waters of nuclear physics and the Unconscious.

EMMA

Ah, yes. Energy equals mass times the speed of light, squared.

TONI

Nothing in the Universe is static.

EMMA

In the language of physics, the atom. In the language of the psyche, the symbol. With Dr. Jung and his guests, I do a great deal of listening, but in reality there are few people I can talk to. I was one year your junior when I married Dr. Jung. He caught his first glimpse of me as a girl of seventeen, descending the staircase, in my parents' home. He said later he knew in that instant I would be his wife. His shyness around women was so great, it was four years before we married. Our wedding was a joyous and spiritual event. Such promise. I made it clear to him I wanted to pursue a life of the mind within the marriage. I have long been fascinated with the Legend of the Holy Grail.

11

TONI

You are writing a book.

EMMA

By spells. I began research. Then our first daughter came, and the next, the next, then our son.

TONI

Marriage has been a mixed blessing for you.

EMMA

I am devoted to my husband and his work. I relish my time with the children—fishing, singing, making mud cakes, yet, I grow impatient to pursue an intellectual life.

TONI

You are suffering.

EMMA

I have so much.

TONI

Do you?

EMMA

How can you know of my world? I must keep all of this going. My husband is one of the great minds. You see that, do you not?

TONI

Were we not speaking of your mind?

EMMA

There will be time. And what of your aspirations, Fraulein?

TONI

You divert, Frau Jung.

EMMA

I will not tolerate any further discussion of my mind, or my marriage.

TONI

I trespassed.

EMMA

I invited it. Good day, Fraulein.

TONI

Can you not work on your book when the children are asleep? You must finish it, or there will never be an end to your suffering.

Emma turns to regard Toni. They hold each other's eyes.

EMMA exits.

MUSIC.

TONI addresses the audience, as she speaks to Jung.

TONI

Something is happening, Dr. Jung. A lightness has come over me, a feeling I have not had since I was a child. I wake each morning to a new adventure. Run, like an antelope, to the library in search of undiscovered wonders for our research. I am well aware these are not the texts you sent me for. I use my own mind and follow it's counsel. Is that not the goal of analysis? Forgive my amusement, but it is a rare sight indeed to see your jaw drop open like a great whale ready to swallow his supper! There is method in my madness.

I bring you texts of the great spiritual traditions of the East: The Hindu BHAGAVAD GITA, writings on the world of Siddharta, the Buddha. The mind of the East has great relevance for your psychology. The Atman, the God within. I have no power to read your mind. You think I do? Then it is an equal exchange, for when I was your analysand, you certainly read mine! You see me as your teacher? Surely you elevate me beyond reason. No? Then I accept the position.

MUSIC.

TONI exits.

EMMA enters, sits at her table, reviewing a letter.

EMMA

Dear Dr. Freud, I was astonished at the exchange during our chance meeting en route to the Weimar conference. You tell me that your children are your "one true joy." Your marriage, you say, has been "amortized" and there is nothing left but for you to die. I cannot believe you are speaking of your own relations, and need to ask if you mean to imply something is amiss between myself and Carl. It is true women flock to him—a thousand virgins, longing for reflected brilliance by gazing like erotic lambs into his eyes. I told you I threatened to divorce him over the Spielrein woman. The latest disciple is this young girl who comes for analysis daily, but she is a studious, asexual sort of person. Not one of the Aphrodite-types who engender such appeal.

(aside)

If I am honest with myself, I must admit that Fraulein Wolff Bears some resemblance to Sabina Spielrein, as intellectual, not as mentally distraught, a certain haunting quality in both of them.I am not comforted by this revelation. . .

(returning to review of the letter)

No, for my own marriage, I anticipate I will be able to forge a union of sexual passion and common intellectual interests, when the children are older. Can you not aspire to this with your wife as well, my dear Dr. Freud?

TONI enters. They are each in their own world, unaware of each other, EMMA reviewing her letters to Freud, TONI speaking to Jung as she addresses the audience.

TONI

Dr. Jung, train me to be an analyst. You have done so already? Of course. My own analysis, critical, lest the feelings of the patient dominate the psyche of the analyst, and vice-versa. I believe you have some experience with this "vice-versa"? Forgive me. An indelicate question. I have heard rumors. A young Jewish patient. Your first analysand? Fraulein Spielrein. Is she still in love with you? Are you still in love with her? I am far too bold. Yet you cannot blame me for having curiosity, from a purely theoretical point of view. Am I correct, or is there a faraway look in your eyes, Dr. Jung? Do you still dream of Fraulein Spielrein? Would you tell me if you did? I think not.

EMMA

Professor Freud, forgive my brazen candor. With all due respect, I am most proud, of course, that you have chosen my husband as you intellectual heir, but I must inquire why you persist to look upon Carl with a father's feeling? I think it is an error on your part to see my husband as the follower and "fulfiller" of your analytic model. You are 56 years old, still many good years left. Why do you behave like an old man, so eager to pass on the reins of succession—and must my husband conform to your theories so precisely, when he is robustly developing his own? Don't be angry with me for this meddling, with warm love and veneration,—Emma.

TONI

At this moment, if I were to make of you a laboratory subject, I would ask what is troubling your mind so deeply, Dr. Jung? Do you think I have not noticed you converse with the air? The very bushes answer back in the voice of Sigmund Freud. No? If not Freud, who is it who speaks to you? You hear voices. Visions of an Old Man with wings. It does not frighten me. Look at me. No, this is not time to ring for a cognac. I do not know what Frau Jung is preparing for your dinner. The Old Man is calling to you to enter the depths of your own Unconscious. Yes, I can see into the inner recesses of your mind. I know what you're thinking before you do. This is about your courage, Dr. Jung. Do you have the courage to face the truth of your own nature?

MUSIC.

TONI exits.

EMMA puts away the letters, takes out a loaf of bread.

TONI enters.

TONI

The smell of warm bread—

EMMA

> Eck, you are always sneaking up on me, Fraulein Wolff.

TONI

> Canisters of flour, bricks of cheese, crimson roses. Is this "your place" in the house?

EMMA

> Every place is my place in this house. Sit down Fraulein - have some bread.

TONI

> I am quite famished, thank you.

TONI devours the bread.

EMMA

> Does my husband never feed you, in the long hours of research?

TONI

> Eating is for mortals.

EMMA

> Merely by reading mythology you ascend Olympus? Quite a feat.

TONI

> It is a danger—to feel so intimate with the gods. One can lose ones' shoes.

EMMA

> I am grateful to you for taking the time to help my husband in his archeology of consciousness. I often performed his library bidding, before our first child was born.

TONI

This bread is the food of the gods. Thank you.

EMMA

I was conversing with a friend who knows your mother. She spoke of your fine abilities as a poet, a story writer. I would be delighted to read some of your work.

TONI

You are a lover of literature?

EMMA

More like a fair weather friend. I attempted ANNA KARENINA. That was enough. Your work is another matter. You have become such a frequent presence, I simply want to know you better.

TONI

I read my poetry and think, "This does not compare to a Summer's Day"—or even to the lesser poets. And my fiction is a poor Swiss version of Jane Austen's genius.

EMMA

My husband would say you are giving sway to a "sniping god" within who wants to keep you from your intended calling.

TONI

Perhaps. But I know better than either of you the nature of my aspirations, and the limits of my art.

EMMA

Now that you are sated, I sense you are eager to go. A moment, please. I have been curious to ask if my

husband has mentioned his relations with Sigmund
Freud.

TONI

He "mentioned" his epic annoyance when he
discovered your clandestine correspondence with
Freud.

EMMA

He told you of this?

TONI

I must go—

EMMA

Nonsense. Have some cheese. What did he say?

TONI

He found the envelope, addressed to you, in Freud's
handwriting.With all due respect, Frau Jung, you
cannot bring them back together. Jung refutes Freud's
construct of the sexual drive as the center of human
motivation, envisioning a larger canvas for the human
soul.

EMMA

Carl is mocked for it: "Mystic" "Heretic". I do not
care if my husband is annoyed with me. It is my right
as the patron of his practice, the wealth supporting
this family—to fight for legitimacy in the world's
eyes.

TONI

Not if it runs afoul of his integrity.

EMMA

It is fine for you to trumpet heresy. What have you
to lose? I have children, a family name to protect.

Since his falling out with Freud, he walks through the garden at all hours of the day and night, mumbling to spirits.

TONI

In order to validate his theories, he feels he must enter his own Unconscious. I too see the peril in it, but do you not see it is a fantastic voyage? He likens it to landing on the Moon.

EMMA

Of course I see it. He journeys to the Infinite not in death, but as a living human being! This has great significance, but without Freud—

TONI

Meddling with Freud will not sew these disparate minds back together.

EMMA

I do not want him to do it alone—

TONI

He is not alone. He has asked me to serve as his analyst.

EMMA

You?

TONI

Yes. Me. I know you see me as a mere slip of a girl. But apparently, there are older, wiser voices inside of me. I often astonish myself, with what comes out, seemingly unbidden. I must get back to him. He asked me to bring some of your bread.

EMMA

> Take a whole loaf, a brick of cheese, and for you, my
> husband's analyst, a rose.

MUSIC.

TONI takes the bread, cheese, the rose and exits.

*EMMA moves into another space, addressing the audience as she
speaks to Jung.*

EMMA

> Carl, why do you choose this girl to be your guide
> through your darkest hours? Separate? She is separate
> from our family in name only. You spend all your
> days, into the nights with her. I want to slap your
> face. This is the greatest infidelity. I have undergone
> analysis with you. I am trained to do this work. I am
> your wife. If you struggle on the brink of madness,
> it is I who should be with you, not this child! You so
> value our blessed Swiss life, our time apart with the
> children? I do not believe you. You bring out your old
> charm to smooth over the fact that you have passed
> me over for Toni Wolff ! Is this some aspect of your
> madness, or are you capable of a cruelty I could not
> have imagined? Tears? Are they truly from your heart,
> or from some crocodile? You will go insane if I am
> not beside you? So I am Mother Earth, rooting you in
> this simple, ordinary, blessed Swiss life?I do not mean
> to mock you. I am angry. I am deeply hurt. Yes, I
> want to be both your Mother Earth and your analyst.
> Why not? You are confused enough? I am to be your
> touchstone in the outer world, and Toni Wolff is to
> excavate the inner one. Do I have a choice?

MUSIC.

21

EMMA moves to The Garden, sits. TONI enters.

TONI

You've been waiting.

EMMA

How is he?

TONI

Asleep. At last. He writes furiously in his notebook.
The paintings emerge.

EMMA

Would he not benefit from a hospital?

TONI

I have asked him. He says he will not be so far away
from you and the children.

EMMA

I know you are doing everything you can. I worry
that these visions will overtake him, and he will be
beyond all of us.

TONI

No moon tonight. Pity. I assume you do not have a
cigarette—

EMMA

Will you sleep on the divan tonight?

TONI

I must go home. My mother worries after my health.
She does not understand. You are to have another
child.

EMMA

He crawls in bed at night and molds his large hands

to my belly.—"Making life is the only certainty, Emma," he whispers, "the only human way to laugh at death".

TONI

You are happy, to be with child?

EMMA

At my age? I feel the weight of the infinite in my womb.

(beat)

Have you ever felt the movement of an unborn child?

TONI

Such things are quite foreign to me.

EMMA reaches for TONI'S hand. TONI stiffens, but gradually allows EMMA to place her hand on EMMA'S belly. EMMA reacts to the movement of the child. TONI feels it too, then moves away, touching her own belly, brushing her breast.

Thank you, Frau Jung. You bring me, as always, into the world of touch, of the senses. It is beautiful. My intuition tells me this is a girl.

EMMA weeps.

He is getting better.

EMMA

Thank you, Fraulein.

Beat. MUSIC.

EMMA exits.

TONI moves down close to the audience, looking out as if through a vast picture window.

TONI

> Jung, the ocean. In this moment, I would trade the mighty Alps for one stretch of such coastline. The fire of the sky reflected in the water: crimson, gold. It was thrilling for me to be here as you read your paper—the International Community shocked but intrigued with your ideas of universal symbols in the Unconscious. I seem to come alive away from Switzerland? Perhaps it is the receptive faces of your colleagues. I, your protégé, taken quite seriously, despite my age and sex. My Italian is wanting. Can we not go to London? Your new daughter is beautiful, is she not? Do not whine at me that she is not a son! It is your duty as her father to change the fossil Swiss laws so your daughters have some political power. Your wife is done with child bearing, but she does not have to move into a separate bedroom if she will consider other methods of curtailing pregnancy. I say this to you because it is true. Are so committed to this idea of yourself: "Carl Gustave Jung, the conventional man?" I know better. Is it possible you do not know what is in my heart? Come to me.

Beat. MUSIC.

TONI exits.

EMMA enters, sits in The Garden.

TONI enters.

TONI

> By the Heavens!

24

EMMA

Now it is I who startle you.

TONI

You have been waiting.

EMMA

I put Lil down for a nap. At four weeks she will not sleep long.

TONI

It gives you joy, to be a mother again?

EMMA

She is beautiful.

TONI

So I have heard. I have not seen her yet.

EMMA

You have been busy.

TONI

We are coming to a new awakening in the work.

EMMA

You seem much altered since the sojourn to Ravenna with my husband.

TONI

I admit I took the liberty to bask in the Italian sun, baking my cheeks to a golden brown.

EMMA

Indeed? To me they seem quite crimson. I speak of a rather more substantial "liberty"—the way you move about with such aplomb in your new Italian silks.

TONI

—They know far more of fashion than we—

EMMA

—this new way of wearing your hair—

TONI

—All the Italian women do so, with a flair—

EMMA

—a lilt of laughter coming from Carl's study—

TONI

—the joy of intellectual conquest—

EMMA

Carl seems to have caught this "liberty" as well. I find him teaching Franz to whistle. Carl himself did not know how, before he lay with you.

TONI

You hate me.

EMMA

Foolish girl. There have been others. There will be more, after he is done with you.

TONI

I am no idle tryst, Frau Jung.

EMMA

This man held your darkness in his hands.

TONI

And I hold his.

EMMA

You are playing with loaded pistols, both of you!

TONI

And you would have the keeping of the firearms?

EMMA

I would have you out of my life.

TONI

I will stay.

EMMA

Have you no thought of propriety?

TONI

In this I do not.

EMMA

Where do you come from, that you can make up your own rules?

TONI

I am not without feelings. I see this is very hard for you.

EMMA

Forgive me if I mistrust what you "see."

TONI

I hold no malice for you. I understand that Jung requires his life with you and the children. You create for him the respectable Swiss family. More than that, a harmonious one—

EMMA

You would destroy this "harmony"?

TONI

I do not aspire to take your place. My life with him inhabits a realm, apart—

EMMA

Hah! Your life with him is not "apart" from us. You are always underfoot! In my kitchen, at my dinner table——

TONI

I will absent myself from the weekday meals, if you desire, but you cannot restrict our colloquy throughout the house, our walks around the lake——

EMMA

Stay out of my kitchen. If you and my husband are hungry, he must be the one to come down and ask for bread.

TONI

I will comply with your conditions.

EMMA

You are not the woman I thought you were.

TONI

From our first meeting, I sensed your kindness, the power of your mind, and how profoundly you underestimated me.

EMMA

I knew you were unconventional. I accepted, even admired it. I did not know it extended to throwing off all moral codes and making of yourself a Salome in my own house.

TONI

I am a woman, with all a woman's needs, desires, weaknesses.

EMMA

And will you have his babies?

TONI

> Do not be absurd. I have concluded that the cervical
> cap is the most effective device in pregnancy
> prevention, well documented by French artists and
> prostitutes. If our situations were reversed, would
> you honestly cry, "Oh but he is married, and walk
> away!"

EMMA

> I would give my soul to have what you have: his mind,
> his heart, his loins, on a platter.

TONI

> How brave you are, to confess this to me.

EMMA

> Out of my garden. Out!

TONI does not move. The women regard each other.

MUSIC.

TONI exits.

EMMA addresses the audience, as she speaks to Jung.

EMMA

> Carl, our Lil, thrives. She nurses like a piglet. My
> nipples are quite sore. I am aware of your concern—
> your mother buried four stillborn before you arrived:
> the miracle birth. I am not your mother. Put down
> your pen and look at me, Carl. How if I take my four
> girls and your son and be done with you. I will not
> be blackmailed by this stone-age Swiss law that gives
> the husband ownership of the wife's fortune. I will
> "manage." That is none of your affair. It is not my fault
> your mother spent her life in mental hospitals. Why

should I suffer because you never got enough breast? You cannot live without us? Can you live without Toni Wolff? I am well aware she is your analyst, your "Anima": the flesh and blood image of your feminine soul. So you must possess her. Poor girl. Where will she go when you are done with her? Enough of this. Tell me of your work. The Psychological Congress? England. I would go as your professional colleague, not simply the illustrious doctor's wife? As my life is consumed with breast milk, it will nourish my mind to learn what scientific discoveries you have made from your visions and dreams. The three of us? Toni Wolff is to join us in this and all future conferences? You mean to push me away. To banish me to a corner where all I am is a loving wife and mother. Though I burn with humiliation, I will go with you, and your Toni Wolff.

MUSIC.

EMMA exits.

TONI enters, looks out to the audience as she addresses Jung.

TONI

Jung. Full moon through the Swiss pine. Can you not hear it, the guns, all the way from Germany? Are we not fiddling while Rome burns? If our work is to be moral, it must go beyond your images and dreams, into the psyche of the world. Yes, there are days I long to don a uniform and pour my blood onto the battlefield at Gallipoli, but that is puffery. In opening my own analytic practice, I am making a commitment to individual development. The goal of our work? To impregnate the violence of the world with consciousness, so that the only enemy we fight is the crucible of our own darkness. God? He longs for a relationship with us, as fully as we do with him. Not only the patriarchal God of the West, but the feminine goddess of the East, omnipresent inside of us, in a rock, a leaf, the reflection in your eyeglasses of the surface of the Lake. And more mysteries I cannot distill for you in a small, round cup. Of this there is no mystery. Carl Gustave, you are my gold, my soul, my love.

MUSIC.

FADE OUT

ACT TWO

MUSIC in the darkness

LIGHTS UP on EMMA in her kitchen. TONI enters

TONI

The fog is lifting off the Lake.

EMMA

Is it? I see new clouds settling in.

TONI

It feels less humid.

EMMA

To me it seems more so.

TONI

You wanted to see me?

EMMA

Yes. Please, have some tea with ice and mint.
A biscuit.

TONI

Thank you, Frau Jung.

EMMA

I wonder you stay so slender. It must be the horse race pace at which you work.

TONI

We feel the pressure of time. So much yet to discover!
I could not believe it when he told me Lil—the "baby"
will be sixteen. She is lovely. Congratulations.

EMMA

Thank you. I asked to meet with you on a matter of
an intellectual nature.

TONI

I am delighted to hear it. One would hope you and I can put our "feeling function" into a bottle and seal the cork.

EMMA

A fine aspiration, at least for the next twenty minutes.

TONI

What matter is burning a hole in your brain?

EMMA

I have opened my own analytic practice.

TONI

I am well aware. I wanted to send you roses to commemorate the occasion, but could not find a thornless variety. I have no doubt you will be a fine analyst and help a great many people.

EMMA

Thank you.

TONI

You are welcome.

EMMA

I have noticed a pattern among the women I see, something quite dramatic, a current, a theme, running in a torrent beneath the surface of their lives—these are women of my age, some even older, whose children are grown or nearly grown. They desire to have an intellectual or artistic life of their own, yet they are saddled with men who take to the bottle, or refuse gainful employment, living off their wives' fortune.

TONI

> A story you know well.

EMMA

> Chide me if you will, this is different. Carl could live comfortably now on his own economy, if he would only charge these wealthy Americans a proper fee! No—what I see in these women is a depletion within themselves—a lack of confidence, infidelity to the Self, projecting their wounded creative drive into these little men! This has something to do with the Animus. I go to Carl and he waxes on and on about the Anima, the feminine soul of a man, but comes up short in helping me understand the Animus problem in women.

TONI

> It is very great. I see it in my analysands as well.

EMMA

> I am attempting to write about it. Writing seems the only way I can really wrestle the meaning out of it. Could you talk to me of your own experience, with the Animus?

TONI

> If I were to describe it as if my Animus were a character in mythology, I would tell you wondrous tales of Chiron, the wounded healer—a centaur —half man, half horse—When I was healing from my depression, he was my guide, pulling me onto his horse back. I felt his healing energy as we road through green fields, my hair loose and flying behind us, my arms wrapped around his bare chest. He carried me until the melancholy lifted.

EMMA

My analysands do not dream of powerful gods, but of houses in ruin, towers falling, babies scattered on the lawn.

TONI

They must take back the projection from their husbands and heal their own wounded inner man.

EMMA

And to do that—

TONI

You want a recipe!

EMMA

Of course—a bit of flour, two parts yeast, a dash of dream interpretation.

TONI

Sit with them in the silence, allow an image, a memory, a question to emerge—

EMMA

In dreams the Animus often makes his first appearance as a little boy.

TONI

Yes, and the dialogue is critical, between the conscious mind of the woman, and her inner "boy."

EMMA

The Animus grows up as this relationship matures.

TONI

Until the dream when the adult woman mates with her adult inner man. A sexual symbol, for a spiritual act.

EMMA

> Modesty forbids this, yet I must tell you: it has happened to me as well! It began as soon as I start writing my essay, ANIMUS AND ANIMA. It seemed that in a dream, I walk into the kitchen through a new door. There stands a man. I recognize at once, —"Tolstoy!" I shout—"You did not like ANNA KARENINA." he says. "Forgive me, Leo, it was such a very long book, and I could not feel kindly toward the heroine, an adulteress." "But this is precisely your course, my dearest Emma"—he cries, throwing me onto the kitchen table, thrusting parsnips and potatoes to the four winds as he takes me. I am awash in passion and feel not a jot of shame!

TONI

> It is infidelity, for when a woman mates with her Animus, it changes her relationship with the exterior man in her life.

EMMA

> Precisely. Now I say to Carl, "I am so sorry I cannot play pool with you this evening, I must write."

TONI

> Wifely duties pushed aside.

EMMA

> When I have attempted to write in the past, I tried to write as he writes, think as he thinks, then I toss it away as second hand nonsense. This work belongs only to me, and Tolstoy.

TONI

> Chiron told me, "Do not quote Jung to your analysands. Listen to the woman's voice within you. That is the only recipe."

EMMA

> I have missed it, talking woman to woman, with you.

TONI

> I have enjoyed this too, Frau Jung. We should relish it. The Genii does not stay happily in the bottle for long.

EMMA

> Indeed
>
> *(lifting her tea cup)*
>
> To Chiron.

TONI

> To Leo!
>
> *They toast.*

MUSIC.

EMMA exits.

TONI moves into The Garden, sits.

EMMA *(off stage)*

> Franz, you have devoured enough berries for an army—let the grand baby pick some. I need 3 full pails to make enough pies for this brood!

EMMA enters.

> Toni Wolff. What has happened? You look as you did when you stumbled into my garden 20 years ago.

TONI cannot speak. EMMA sits next to her.

> A return of the melancholy? This must be, what, the 25th anniversary of your father's death? Some new event, of a delicate nature?

TONI is silent.

> How old are you now, 46?
> Still slender, still lovely, still, no doubt, his "Anima"—

TONI looks at EMMA at last.

> No? There are certainly many aspiring would-be-analysts throwing themselves at his head. One of them landed in his bedroom?

TONI

> No.

EMMA

> Something of a more serious nature.

TONI cannot speak.

> A mind has come. A new woman of fierce intellect, to knock you off the golden pedestal you have straddled, these two decades. Is it Barbara Hannah, the British swan?

TONI

> No, she is devoted to me. It is not she who is the source of my grief.

EMMA

> Ah, Of course. The friend of your nephew, the teenager you picked up at the train station and delivered to Carl's door. Marie Louise Von Franz.

TONI

> She is a girl of 18, a disciple who will do anything he asks of her. I see it now—last year, our trip to Rome. He prowled the libraries for texts on Alchemy— Hacks and quacks from the Middle Ages, melting lead into "gold"—"Why on earth does this interest you?"

I asked him—"This is what I have been searching for, Toni. The foundation in the ancient world for my theories of Individuation!" "You are insane!" I told him, "This heresy does not belong in you science of psychology!" Now—Von Franz is off to the library, pronouncing Alchemy 'the Ultimate New Science of Psychology'—"She will be my lieutenant" he said, "I have no more use for you, Toni Wolff!"

EMMA

I am stunned. I would not have though him capable of such behavior. Surely this is not permanent banishment.

TONI

I feel it in my bones. He will not back down. He is too obsessed with this 'Alchemical Revolution' —"How ironic," I told him, "I cannot follow you in this because I am too Individuated!" If I had said "Alchemy, what genius," he would never have replaced me with this child!

EMMA

You have the honor of standing in your own truth.

TONI

What a price I pay for it!

EMMA

Joan of Arc comes to mind.

TONI

Joan of Arc be damned. This was my whole life.

EMMA

It is no shame, to feel.

TONI

I am mortified by my woman's weakness. Yet, here I am. I read your book, ANIMUS AND ANIMA, like a crisp translation of Tolstoy's prose.

EMMA

You alone on earth know to characterize it thus!

TONI

I was gratified that you cited the the modern birth control movement as a boon for all womankind.

EMMA

I should have embraced the risks and indelicacies of the cervical cap decades ago! I was most impressed by your paper, STRUCTURAL FORMS OF THE FEMININE PSYCHE. You have transformed the Psychological Club of Zürich into a vital intellectual force.

TONI

He dare not rob me of my presidency.

EMMA

I have long thought he should credit your work on psychological types.

TONI

Then you would be owed some acclaim as well, for I came to my formulation of the Sensate Type quite drunk on the smell of your fresh baked bread.

EMMA

How very unexpected. I should be doing a dance to see you now in my shoes, suffering, even as I suffered when he chose you over me. Instead I feel a depth of empathy for you, Toni Wolff.

TONI

God help me. Now I know how you felt, watching me trot about in front of you, "He likes my mind better than yours." What a consummate ass I was— What a consummate ass I am. I am not humbled by this grief—I am a queen without a country, licking my wounds, howling at the moon. A quarter century since my father's death—once again, I stare down, into a shattered darkness. But to whom do I turn? I cannot go for analysis with Dr. Carl Gustave Jung. And, why do I speak of this to you, Emma Jung, of all souls on this earth?

EMMA

Because I am here.

MUSIC.

TONI exits.

EMMA moves into "The Bedroom", awakes with a SCREAM.

EMMA

Carl, you are here. A dream. Our doorway painted with Swastikas, in blood, the blood of the Jews. Freud's head on a stick. You are hell bent on destroying this family. Next time you go to Berlin, there will be real Swastikas on our door. Your 'International Psychological Society' has become a propaganda machine for the Third Reich. Everyone knows this but you. You did such a fine job portraying the Jews as the "Shadow" of the German psyche, Hitler twists it and uses your words to justify his persecution of the "Shadow race." The works of Freud and Adler are burned in Berlin, because you wrote, "Jewish Psychiatry is thoroughly unsatisfying to the German mentality. "You are correct. Nazi's chop your words out of context. That is what dictators do. You must renounce Hitler. Resign this puppet presidency. What is it you are hiding, from me, from yourself? I am frightened, Carl. I can feel the walls of Europe closing in around us. No. I do not know if I want you to hold me in this darkness, or come into my bed after all these years. No. I will never forgive you. The shoe is on the other foot. Can I open my heart to you? I do not know, Carl, I do not know.

MUSIC.

EMMA exits.

TONI enters, addressing the audience as Jung.

TONI

Carl Gustave Jung, look at me. I know what you have done. Vladimir Rosenbaum. The International Congress in Berlin. Rosenbaum came to your rescue. Rosenbaum wrote the statutes that saved the lives of Jewish psychiatrists throughout Europe. A man of great courage and principle. Do you hate him because he stands before the world against dictatorship and you don't? He had the courage to join the underground forces against Franco. A criminal? Only under this myopic Swiss Law. What of Universal human justice? He came to you, straight from prison, his life in ruin. You sent him away with nothing. He was your analysand. Your friend. You are a coward, terrified your fine Swiss neighbors, will call you friend of a Jew. A switch flips inside your heart. You exterminated Rosenbaum as you exterminated me. I look at you, I do not see Carl Gustave Jung, the man I love, my analyst, friend. I see only the Exterminator.

MUSIC.

TONI exits.

EMMA enters, sits in The Garden.

TONI enters.

TONI

I have been searching for you, Frau Jung. The afternoon sun, reflected in the Lake, like the skin of a peach. Blessed silence. The radio seems to follow me, even in my dreams.

EMMA

It follows all of us, since Hitler invaded Poland. You heard?

TONI

Freud is dead.

EMMA

He died in England. Far away from the Third Reich. A free man. It seems the snow has melted from the Alps, the peaks barren of life, now he is gone.

TONI

I met him only briefly.

EMMA

Good. You would have had them both in love with you! When Freud arrived in London, Carl assured me he sent a telegram, congratulating him. I discovered later the missive never reached England. I chided Carl,—"What is this, a Freudian slip?" He wrung his hands and swore to me he gave the telegram to the clerk. It is of no consequence now.

TONI

I wish I had known Sigmund Freud.

EMMA

I always felt visible in his eyes. That he saw in me a woman Carl was blind to.

TONI

Forgive me if I speak out of school, but did your relationship with Freud border on intimacy?

EMMA

Not in the physical sense, but perhaps you above all people know that a man's mind is by far his most sensual organ.

TONI

For me it has always been so.

EMMA

My mind opened to meet the challenge of his.

TONI

And vice-versa.

EMMA

It was never stated, yet I always felt if his wife succumbed to sudden illness and Carl fell into the Lake and drowned, Freud would be at my doorstep with a large bouquet.

TONI

You regret this did not come to pass?

EMMA

Fraulein, I want to gather some people together, to share our memories, of Freud and his work. Would you care to assist me?

TONI

> It will be an honor, Frau Jung.

MUSIC.

TONI and EMMA exit.

EMMA enters, makes bread in the kitchen.

TONI enters.

TONI

> The smell of fresh baked bread. I do miss the flowers.

EMMA

> So do I. Whoever thought there would be a law directing all Swiss citizens to plant every square inch of land in food crops, banishing the flowers.

TONI

> *(saluting)*

> Frau Jung, you are doing your duty.

EMMA

> *(returning the salute)*

> Fraulein Wolff. Stunning uniform.

TONI

> Women's Intellectual Auxiliary, at your service.

EMMA

> Intellectual?

TONI

> Not my designation. I practice driving an ambulance, in case we are invaded. I put in for carrier pigeon reconnaissance, but those jobs were taken.

EMMA

Pity. Won't you have some tea?

TONI

Only if you toss in bread and honey.

EMMA

Lucky you did not ask for sausage.

TONI

Meat is not required to sustain human life.

EMMA

But one wants a choice, not a blockade! I should not whine—we can grow our provisions, unlike most of Europe.

TONI

I am ravenous!

EMMA

Do they not feed you, in the barracks?

TONI

Indistinguishable things in tins. We need more recruits, Frau Jung. The Germans are bombing London as we sit here sipping English Breakfast Tea. Join us.

EMMA

Fraulein Wolff, I admire your zeal for the Cause, but I approach my 60th year. I find myself running a farm, packing potatoes to send to refugees—

TONI

The servants can do that.

EMMA

Perhaps you are unaware I command a commune

here of daughters, 5 grandchildren, and a pregnant daughter-in-law, now Franz and all the husbands serve in the military. We live from day to day, awaiting invasion. I have rented a pension in the mountains. Daily I urge Carl to go with us in preemptive evacuation. His name is on the Nazi Black list to be arrested, incarcerated, or exterminated.

TONI

A triumph for him.

EMMA

I am more deeply proud of him than at any time in our marriage. He has found his voice, his goodness, and speaks out against this evil to all the world.

TONI

It is a cause for celebration.

EMMA

More bread?

TONI

Thank you, no, but I am desperate for a cigarette.

EMMA

You are welcome to step outside and puff on the potatoes.

TONI

A snifter of brandy?

EMMA

Have some more tea, Fraulein of the Women's Intellectual Auxiliary.

TONI

The first time I put on this uniform, I looked at

myself in the glass, I saw a new woman, part of
something much larger: this Archetypal polarity of
"Right" against "Evil."

EMMA

You are more vulnerable to the grandiose than I
feared.

TONI

Certainly less individuated than I had thought.
Suddenly I am not Toni Wolff, analyst, woman with
an inner life, etc. I am Switzerland. Ah, Frau Jung,
there is a story that when the goddess of Love fell
in love with the god of War, all the gods came down
to make judgment of this dangerous union, but the
goddesses stayed home, crying they are too delicate
to look upon the carnal scene. Perhaps you could
write about it, this phenomenon of the goddesses in
hiding? No? No time to lift your pen?

EMMA

Sometimes late at night, after the last grandchild is in
bed, I have a few moments to think of the hours I
would like to spend in quiet reflection, or in talking
with someone willing to know my thoughts, my
heart—

TONI

How alone you feel.

EMMA

Yes. How alone

TONI

Even Tolstoy has gone off to war?

EMMA

I miss him so. I miss the energy, the passion, the Emma I was when I could carve out time of my own.

TONI

Your personal Holy Grail.

EMMA

The life of a mother, now a grandmother, has been my essence. I cannot imagine who I would be devoid of home and children. Perhaps I ask too much, that I should also embody in one lifetime this other dimension.

TONI

Not everyone can do it. Not everyone wants to. But for you, Emma Jung, such embodiment is not only possible. It is necessary.

TONI notices something out the window.

She is leaving for the day—

EMMA

Marie Louise Von Franz.

TONI

Going home to Barbara Hannah.

EMMA

My husband was truly inspired, to recommend they live together.

TONI

He always said, "Without relationship, this work is but a froth of theory."

EMMA

And how is it with you, Fraulein Wolff? Your reputation as an analyst is without parallel. In Zürich they say, "If you want to be educated, go to Carl Jung. If you want to be transformed, see Toni Wolff."

TONI

Thank you. It is the honor of my life to do this work.

EMMA

So much receiving the pain of others. Who listens to you?

TONI

Frau Jung, I fear if I put one toe into this territory, we will be here until midnight, and all the soft napkins in your cupboards will not absorb all the tears.

EMMA

We should dig a great well, here in the center of my kitchen, to receive all our mourning.

TONI

We can weep, and drink from it.

EMMA

Take a bath in it.

TONI

For all our sorrows, all our sins. God forgive me. I excoriated him for Rosenbaum, then what do I do? Limit the membership of Jewish psychiatrists in the Zürich Psychological Club. I told myself it was to protect the profession of our natural born Swiss. But is that the truth of it? Do I not look away when I see a Jew walking toward me on the street?

EMMA

    There is shadow in all of us.

TONI

    Rather less of it in you, Frau Jung.

EMMA

    You would employ a measuring cup, Fraulein?

TONI

    I make only one request: a loaf of your bread, for the barracks.

EMMA gives TONI a loaf of bread.

MUSIC.

TONI exits.

EMMA moves into the Hospital Corridor.

TONI enters.

TONI

    He cannot be dying.

EMMA

    The nurse let you in? This is a private family matter.

TONI

    He is not only a private man.

EMMA

    Go home, Fraulein.

TONI

    You must let me in.

EMMA

    You give me orders, Fraulein?

TONI

> I must see him.

EMMA

> You cannot.

TONI

> He wants to see me.

EMMA

> On what authority do you presume this?

TONI

> The conviction of my heart.

EMMA

> This is about his heart, Fraulein. It has nothing to do
> with you.

TONI

> He's had a heart attack.

EMMA

> Clots, lodged in the heart and lungs.

TONI

> I can appreciate how overwrought your must be—

EMMA

> It is not about me, either.

TONI

> It is all about you. He is too weak to say who comes,
> who goes—

EMMA

> Fiction, Fraulein. Must you force me to hurt you?

TONI

What did he say?

EMMA

He asked me to admit no one but Marie Louise Von Franz, our children and grandchildren. No one.

TONI

I do not believe you. Old rivalry rears its head.

EMMA

The "old rivalry" between us is dead, Fraulein. He dreams of me: our first meeting, our intimate life together.

TONI

His heart is broken, he turns to you as a babe to his mother's breast.

EMMA

Fraulein, I am his wife.

TONI

If he dies, my grief will be no less than yours.

EMMA

Even in grieving you construct competition.

TONI

I do not believe you are made of stone.

EMMA

I have him back again. No, I have with him now a true, conscious marriage: a union of mind, body, emotion we have never had before.

Silence.

I hear your thoughts, Fraulein.

TONI

> You presume to read my mind?

EMMA

> As you have always read mine. No. You are wrong.
> I do not achieve this completeness with him only to
> lose him. He will not die. He cannot. Not now.

TONI

> May I sit with you awhile, Frau Jung?

EMMA

> It will not dissolve my will.

TONI

> I know. I do not want you to endure this alone.

EMMA

> Sit, Fraulein. The chairs are hard.

TONI

> *(sits)*
>
> They are indeed, Frau Jung. Thank you.

MUSIC.

EMMA exits. TONI places a chair center stage and opens a writing tablet, addressing the audience.

TONI

> Dear Carl Gustave Jung, I hope this letter finds your
> health improving. While I am loathe to disturb you
> in your vulnerable state, there are some things I feel
> compelled to tell you. I see things quite differently
> now, from my post outside the walls of Eden. Years
> ago, you may recall, my father said to me in a dream,

"People when they live on this earth, they don't know what they have!' I now believe he was speaking of you and me, Carl Gustave. We thrived in our private world of the psyche, but both of us have had difficulty bringing this wondrous reality down to earth. We are talented at analyzing others, but peer through a glass darkly at our own Shadows. I regret that when I was a young woman, I did not have sufficient vision or courage to guide you in confronting your inner "Exterminator." Had I been a giantess of an analyst, I could have helped you do battle with, and tend all the dark, frightened, puffed-up parts of yourself, bringing you into a loving whole. A "you" who did not need to reject parts of yourself, or others. I have paid dearly for this failing, as I became the unwitting victim of it.

(aside)

A giantess of an analyst? What inflation! Yet, I truly believe that is what he needed. Or am I still trying to heal my own wounded Animus, by conjecturing that I could have cured Jung?

(back to the letter)

Carl Gustave, all this being said, I must confess that when I heard you might be dying, all I could see was your face, your body so large it blocks out the sun, your wild laughter. I wept that I might never be in your presence again. I can imagine what my father would say: "Toni Wolff: one who loved, not wisely, but too well." So much I long to ask you, Carl Gustave. Does J. Robert Oppenheimer see the dying victims of Hiroshima in his dreams? Did he see them before he built the Atomic Bomb? If he had, would it have made a difference? What is it we must do, to build something positive in the world, after this long and terrible war?

With all my desire for your full recovery,

Toni

MUSIC.

TONI and EMMA move into the space of an empty house, Gemeindestrasse.

TONI

It is not big enough—

EMMA

Badly needs a coat of paint—

TONI

If we knock down this wall—?

EMMA

A Great Room. Large enough for formal lectures— The C.G. Jung Institute of Zürich.

TONI

The upper floor will do for small symposia—

EMMA

Small classes on select topics—

TONI

The nature of the collective unconscious—

EMMA

Intuition, Sensation—

TONI

Alchemy!

EMMA

You should teach that one!

TONI

Ha! No—you are brilliant: teach what you have turned your back on! Challenge each student to find their own path—

EMMA

Yes! Not the Gospel According to Jung.

TONI

Find your own Inner Tolstoy!

EMMA

Your Inner Chiron!

TONI

This is heresy. We have no university degrees—

EMMA

No formal teacher training—

TONI

We are women. We can't even vote in this country!

EMMA

I don't care! If we are heretics, let the fire begin!

TONI

Could use a throw rug.

(knocks on the floor)

Oak?

EMMA

Solid Swiss hardwood.

TONI

What does it mean, that it is you and I, standing on the boards of this fine old house, improbable mothers of this love child?

EMMA

You fear we will quarrel over the diapering?

TONI

Can you and I work together? There is talk your influence restricted me from the Board.

EMMA

I desire you on the ground floor, Fraulein. Your feet, planted on these sturdy planks, your indispensable mind.

TONI

In times past it has been my disposable mind. I cannot go through that again. I will not.

EMMA

I can give you no guarantee. But if we focus on the care and tending of the child, on what our opposite natures bring into the nursery, what we build here could echo across the world.

TONI

"People are people through other people."

EMMA

Shakespeare?

TONI

South African proverb.

EMMA

> I just got a sensation up the back of my neck.

TONI

> I feel it too. "The future in the instant". That is Shakespeare.

EMMA

> Fraulein, where will we get students to pay for all this?

TONI

> One guess:

TONI/EMMA

> America!

TONI and EMMA move apart, each speaking out to the audience.

EMMA

> I had no idea her command of details—Give Toni Wolff a list of questions, she takes off like a rocket of research—in a day it is done.

TONI

> What skill she has at marshaling resources—put her in the military, she would run circles around General Patton.

EMMA

> She is a wonder to work with.

TONI

> I slip into the back of the room in Frau Jung's course on the Legend of the Holy Grail. A young American student asks a very elementary question. Frau Jung replies, "I don't know the answer to that. I never even thought of the question before!" She then bursts into

laughter—the musical laughter of a young girl, or rather, of a carefree, wise woman. We all join in. I feel a freedom—a gratitude to be alive in this moment, with her.

EMMA

I slip into the back of the room in Fraulein Wolff's class. She does not stand behind a lectern but sits perched on the edge of the desk, like a diver ready to plunge from the board! She gives a case example of an analysand whose husband is involved with another woman. Fraulein Wolff does not join in empathy with the woman's misery, but suggests the analysand invite the other woman to lunch—"For if you got to know her," says Toni Wolff, "you might even like her. Sometimes, if a man's wife is big enough to leap over the hurdle of self pity, she may find that the supposed rival has even helped the marriage." I cannot tell if she sees me in the back of the room, but I am intrigued.

TONI and EMMA come back together, addressing each other.

TONI

What do you think?

EMMA

I think we should form a weekly teacher's club—

TONI

Learn from each other—

EMMA

—Go over what worked that week—

TONI

—what didn't—

EMMA

—what next—

TONI

We start, the rest of the faculty will join.

EMMA

You really must stop smoking. The students mock you.

TONI

Nonsense. They offer me exotic tobacco, from all over the world. Don't scold me for my wanton habits, ask of my visions and dreams.

EMMA

I stand duly rebuked. Tell me wondrous tales of your Animus.

TONI

Chiron has returned. In profile he favors my father, but when he looks at me straight on, his features are quite different: very thick black-rimmed spectacles, eyes gentle. He reaches out, as if to pull me onto his broad equine haunches.

EMMA

Where is he taking you?

TONI

Who knows? It seems enough to contemplate galloping through green fields on a centaur's back.

EMMA

It is lovely, is it not, that we are free of the past? No one here at the Institute has a whiff of the scandal that for many years we were both his wife.

TONI

My God. I did not think I would live to hear such words from your lips.

EMMA

Is it not the truth?

TONI

Indeed. Forgive me. All those years I saw you only as the "other," the enemy, his "real" wife. I did not realize how brutally I diminished you with my projection.

EMMA

And who do you see, now, Fraulein? Who is Emma Jung?

TONI

A woman who is a brilliant teacher, analyst, author—

EMMA

Not my credentials, Fraulein. What do you see?

TONI

Your hand, reaching for mine to feel the movement of your unborn child. Your loving consciousness. Your delight in the "all" of you: the sweetest scented rose, the sharpest thorns.

EMMA

It has come to me too, this awakening, taking down the veils that were so thick between us. How I hated you, Toni Wolff. You became what I had always wanted to be: his analyst, his muse, leading him through his great depression to inspire his greatest creative work. I never saw you as a separate, unique being. I too saw the enemy.

TONI

I, the "Soviet Union" to your "Switzerland."

EMMA

Precisely. Now I am free to see you as you are: one who stands in her own passions, bravely, perhaps rashly, against the moreys of her time.

TONI

He could not have done it, without both of us.

EMMA

Thank you.

TONI

If the world leaders of the future have such powerful women in their lives—or are such powerful women, they will bang their swords into plough shares and study war no more.

EMMA

How you amuse me. There will always be Evil in the world, war and insane dictators.

TONI

Perhaps. Or the goddesses will place their dainty feet upon the earth and cry "Afoul!" of our long love affair with war.

EMMA

I thank God that I have been blessed to know the "all" of you.

TONI

And I, you.

TONI extends her hand. EMMA shakes it.

EMMA

> How soft it is. I have not held your hand these 40 years. Is not that strange?

TONI

> Yours has grown quite rough.

EMMA

> Tomorrow morning, 8:00, we begin our faculty club of two?

TONI

> I will be here.

EMMA turns to go.

TONI

> Emma. Will you do me a personal favor?

EMMA looks back at her.

> Will you teach me to bake bread?

EMMA

> It will be a pleasure, Toni.

MUSIC.

TONI exits.

EMMA moves down, looking out at the audience, speaking to Jung.

EMMA

> Carl. Yes, something has happened. Toni did not come to our meeting this morning. I thought she might have stopped to buy flowers on this first day of Spring. Soon I received the news: Toni Wolff died in the night. Heart attack. I held her hand only yesterday. So soft. You weep for her, your dearest true love. Do not

bother to deny it. I have known, all these years. I can see her now, in my mind's eye, wearing a shimmering gown of aquamarine blue, an angel perched in your Unconscious, whispering, "Carl Gustave Jung, you suffer at my death. How ironic."

EMMA moves down stage, away from "Jung", addresses the audience.

I attend Toni's funeral alone. Carl will not allow the world to see his grief. Looking across the faces of her students, analysands, dear friends, I weep at last. In part the tears are for myself, for it took me forty years to truly know her. I place a rose in her casket, with my recipe for her favorite bread.

TONI enters, stands beside EMMA, addressing the audience.

TONI

Oh, goddesses who made this beautiful earth, how long will you be in hiding? How long? Come forth, so the Alchemy of the new world can begin.

Beat.

MUSIC.

FADE OUT.

ABOUT THE AUTHOR

Elizabeth Clark-Stern is a psychotherapist in private practice in Seattle, Washington. Before embracing this beloved work, she was a professional writer and actor. Her produced plays and teleplays include *All I Could See From Where I Stood, Help Wanted, To See the Elephant, Having Babies II, Nana Sophia's Oasis,* and the documentary *Home From the Eastern Sea. Out of the Shadows: A Story of Toni Wolff and Emma Jung* began as an independent study at Antioch University. Revised some years later, the International Association of Analytical Psychologists invited the original production to perform in South Africa in 2007 with psychoanalyst/professional actor, Rikki Ricard, as Emma Jung, and the author as Toni Wolff.

Learn More about the author at:

www.elizabethclarkstern.com

You might also enjoy reading:

Fisher King Press is pleased to present the following recently published Jungian titles for your consideration:

Farming Soul ISBN 978-1-926715-0-18
Patricia Damery

The Sister from Below ISBN 978-0-9810344-2-3
Naomi Ruth Lowinsky

The Motherline ISBN 978-0-9810344-6-1
Naomi Ruth Lowinsky

The Creative Soul ISBN 978-0-9810344-4-7
Lawrence H. Staples

Guilt with a Twist ISBN 978-0-9776076-4-8
Lawrence H. Staples

Enemy, Cripple, Beggar ISBN 978-0-9776076-7-9
Erel Shalit

Re-Imagining Mary ISBN 978-0-9810344-1-6
Mariann Burke

Divine Madness ISBN 978-1-926715-0-49
John R. Haule

Resurrecting the Unicorn ISBN 978-0-9810344-0-9
Bud Harris

The Father Quest ISBN 978-0-9810344-9-2
Bud Harris

Like Gold Through Fire ISBN 978-0-9810344-5-4
Massimilla and Bud Harris

The Art of Love: The Craft of Relationship
Massimilla and Bud Harris ISBN 978-1-926715-0-25

Learn more about the many worthy publications available for purchase at **www.fisherkingpress.com**

In Canada & the U.S. call
1-800-228-9316
International call
+1-831-238-7799

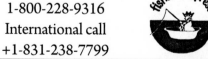

The Creative Soul:
Art and the Quest for Wholeness
a Jungian Perspective by Lawrence H. Staples

ISBN 978-0-9810344-4-7

Who we most deeply are is mirrored in our artistic work. Our need for mirroring simultaneously attracts us to and repels us from our creative callings and relationships. It is one of life's great dilemmas.

Artist's block and lover's block flow from the same pool. Often, we fear deeply the very thing needed to create original art, to experience intimate relationships and to live authentic lives: we are frightened by the impulse to be fully revealed to ourselves, and to others, as this most often entails exposing the unacceptable shadowy aspects of our humanity and risking rejection.

Mirrors in all their manifold guises permit us to safely see and experience ourselves in reflection and become better acquainted with the rejected, ostracized aspects of our personalities. Creative work is one of the few places where we can truly express and witness lost aspects of our authentic selves.

Within us a treasure beckons. This is what we spend our lives pursuing. What slows and distracts us is not the object we long for, but where we search. To find this precious gem, we must eventually return to our own creative spirits.

Topics explored in *The Creative Soul* include:

opposites and creativity — the creative instinct — our unique identity — some elements of creativity —some prerequisites of the creative process — la petite mort — the patriarchal/matriarchal conflict — giving voice to the many lives within — dreams and active imagination as triggers to creativity — creativity as an inner parent — creativity within bounds — the creative gap — the power of small — creativity and independence — art and the quest for wholeness — therapy as art — fear of self-revelation blocks creativity — intimacy and creativity — the importance of mirroring — creativity, guilt, and self-development — creativity and loneliness — life and the tension of opposites

CPSIA information can be obtained at www.ICGtesting.com
Printed in the USA
LVOW07s0048300915

456249LV00001BA/59/P